Junior Science
balancing

Terry Jennings

Illustrations by David Anstey
Gloucester Press
New York · London · Toronto · Sydney

About this book

You can learn many things about balancing in this book. It tells you how things balance, what makes things balance best and how scales work. There are many activities and experiments for you to try. You can find out how to make a balancing bird and doll, and how to make a mobile.

First published in the
United States in 1989 by
Gloucester Press
387 Park Avenue South
New York, NY 10016

ISBN 0 531 17175 2

Library of Congress Catalog
Card Number: 88-83615

This book was designed and produced by BLA
Publishing Limited, TR House, Christopher
Road, East Grinstead, Sussex, England.
A member of the Ling Kee Group
London Hong Kong Taipei Singapore New York

Printed in Spain by Heraclio Fournier, S.A.

Look at the children in the picture. They are keeping steady without falling. They are balancing. One girl is balancing on her head, the other is balancing on a bench and the boy is balancing on a brick.

3

We can balance our bodies. We can also balance things. The children in the picture are balancing things. This boy is balancing a ball on his feet.

This girl is balancing a broom on her hand.

4

This boy is balancing a basket.

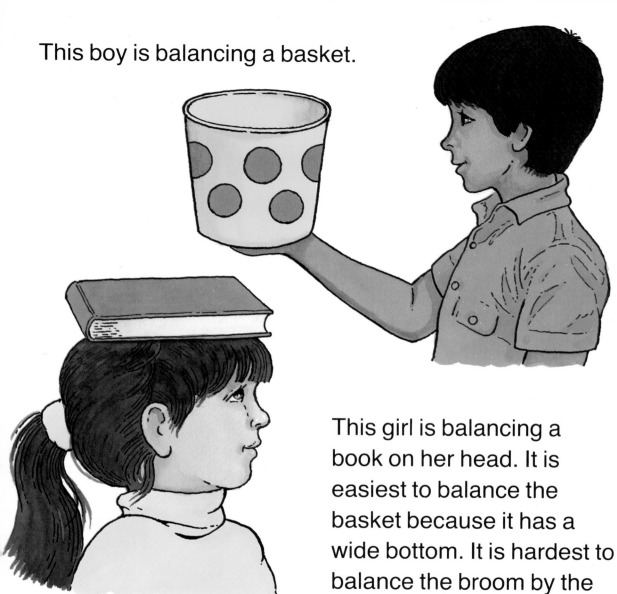

This girl is balancing a book on her head. It is easiest to balance the basket because it has a wide bottom. It is hardest to balance the broom by the handle.

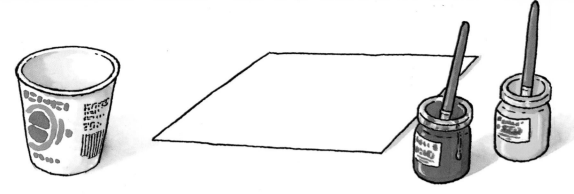

You can make a pencil holder like this. Cover a plastic cup with white paper and paint it. If you put your pencils in it now, the cup would fall over. But you can make the cup balance by putting some modeling clay in the bottom of it.

This boy has two plastic bottles that are the same
size. He put sand in one of the bottles and stood the
bottles side by side. Then he pushed the bottles
over. It was easiest to push over the empty bottle.

Try this experiment. Take
two cans that are the same
size. Put modeling clay in
the bottom of one can and
inside the lid of the other
can. Now place one of the
cans on a book and slowly
lift the cover of the book
until the can slides off.

Now do the same with
the other can. You will see
that the can with the clay at
the top will slide first.

Things balance better when they are heavier at the bottom. This bus is heavier at the bottom. It must be able to tilt a little bit without falling over.

Buses like this are tested to see how far they can tilt without falling over. People can stand downstairs on this bus. But they must not stand upstairs. This would make the bus less balanced.

This girl is riding a bicycle. She has
to balance on it. She can balance
easiest when she rides quickly.
Her sister has a tricycle. It is easier to balance on a
tricycle than on a bicycle. A bicycle only has two
wheels, but a tricycle has three wheels.

These children were playing in the park on the seesaw. Two of them sat at one end of the seesaw and the other sat at the opposite end. The children did not balance.

The two children who were sitting at one end of the seesaw moved. They moved closer to the middle of the seesaw. Now the children balanced.

You can make a toy seesaw like this. Fill a paper cup with sand. Push a needle through the middle of a drinking straw. Then push the needle into the cup to attach the straw to the cup. The seesaw will move easily.

14

Put a paper clip on one side of the seesaw. It will tip down like this.

Put a paper clip on the other side of the seesaw. It will balance.

Now put another paper clip on the seesaw and it will tip like this.

To make the seesaw balance again move the two paper clips toward the middle of the seesaw.

Scales are a kind of seesaw. When two things weigh the same, the scales balance. When one side of the scales tips down, it means this side is heavier.

Look at this picture. The red box is full. The blue box is full too. But the contents of blue box must be heavier than the contents of the red box.

This boy has a set of scales. He put a one pound weight on one side of the scales and a toy car on the other side of the scales. The scales did not balance because the one pound weight was heavier than the toy car. This means that the car must weigh less than one pound.

Big things are not always heavier than small things. The two children are trying to balance a ball and a balloon. The ball weighs more than the balloon, even though the balloon is bigger.

18

You can make a balancing doll. Cut out the doll shape from thin cardboard and color it. Then take a clean egg shell and fill it with modeling clay. Carefully stand the paper doll in the clay. Push the doll with your finger. It will fall over and then stand up again on its own.

You can also make a balancing bird. Draw a bird like this on thick cardboard and cut it out. Put it on the back of a chair. If the bird falls off, attach a piece of clay to its tail. Now it will balance.

Make a mobile. Cut out
some cardboard shapes
and color them. Tie the
shapes to thin sticks like
this.

If one end of a stick hangs down, move the string
along a bit. Then the mobile will balance. Moving air
in the room will make the mobile turn.

Some animals are very good balancers. The pink bird in the picture is a flamingo. It balances on one leg when it sleeps. Many birds sit on telephone wires. They grip the wires with their toes. Their tails and bodies balance them. Kangaroos hop along on two legs. They use their tails for balance.

glossary

Here are the meanings of some words you may have used for the first time in this book.

balance: to keep or make something or somebody steady; to make two things weigh the same.

bicycle: a two wheeled vehicle with pedals which you can ride, sometimes called a bike.

mobile: a hanging decoration that moves in the air.

scales: a weighing machine.

tilt: to make something lean or slope.

tricycle: a vehicle with three wheels and two pedals which you can ride.

index